SUPER SCIENCE FEATS

CELL PHONES

by Nikole Brooks Bethea

Ideas for Parents and Teachers

Pogo Books let children practice reading informational text while introducing them to nonfiction features such as headings, labels, sidebars, maps, and diagrams, as well as a table of contents, glossary, and index.

Carefully leveled text with a strong photo match offers early fluent readers the support they need to succeed.

Before Reading

- "Walk" through the book and point out the various nonfiction features. Ask the student what purpose each feature serves.
- Look at the glossary together. Read and discuss the words.

Read the Book

- Have the child read the book independently.
- Invite him or her to list questions that arise from reading.

After Reading

- Discuss the child's questions. Talk about how he or she might find answers to those questions.
- Prompt the child to think more. Ask: Do you use a cell phone? Have you thought about how cell phones work?

Pogo Books are published by Jump!
5357 Penn Avenue South
Minneapolis, MN 55419
www.jumplibrary.com

Copyright © 2019 Jump!
International copyright reserved in all countries.
No part of this book may be reproduced in any form without written permission from the publisher.

Library of Congress Cataloging-in-Publication Data

Names: Bethea, Nikole Brooks, author.
Title: Cell phones / by Nikole Brooks Bethea.
Description: Minneapolis, MN: Jump, [2018]
Series: Super science feats
"Pogo Books are published by Jump!"
Includes bibliographical references and index.
Identifiers: LCCN 2017054035 (print)
LCCN 2017052905 (ebook)
ISBN 9781624968679 (ebook)
ISBN 9781624968662 (hardcover: alk. paper)
Subjects: LCSH: Cell phones—Juvenile literature.
Technological innovations—Juvenile literature.
Classification: LCC TK6564.4.C45 (print)
LCC TK6564.4.C45 B48 2018 (ebook)
DDC 384.5/3—dc23
LC record available at https://lccn.loc.gov/2017054035

Editor: Kristine Spanier
Book Designer: Michelle Sonnek

Photo Credits: Chris Willson/Alamy, cover (left); photka/Shutterstock, cover (right); psirob/Shutterstock, 1; SKrow/iStock, 3; Ljupco Smokovski/Shutterstock, 4; paulaphoto/Shutterstock, 5; AP Images, 6–7; WENN Ltd/Alamy, 8–9; Akhenaton Images/Shutterstock, 10–11; Poravute Siriphiroon/Shutterstock, 12; Andrey_Popov/Shutterstock, 13; Visuals Stock/Alamy, 14–15; thaikrit/Shutterstock, 16; sirtavelalot/Shutterstock, 17; mbond77/Shutterstock, 18–19; dszc/iStock, 20–21; POM POM/Shutterstock, 23.

Printed in the United States of America at Corporate Graphics in North Mankato, Minnesota.

TABLE OF CONTENTS

CHAPTER 1
Amazing Devices 4

CHAPTER 2
How They Work 12

CHAPTER 3
A World of Networks 16

ACTIVITIES & TOOLS
Try This! 22
Glossary 23
Index 24
To Learn More 24

CHAPTER 1
AMAZING DEVICES

We use cell phones for many things. Games. Pictures. Music. They are amazing.

We use them to call people. And we can use them to check **social media**. Our phones keep us connected. But how do phones connect?

CHAPTER 1 5

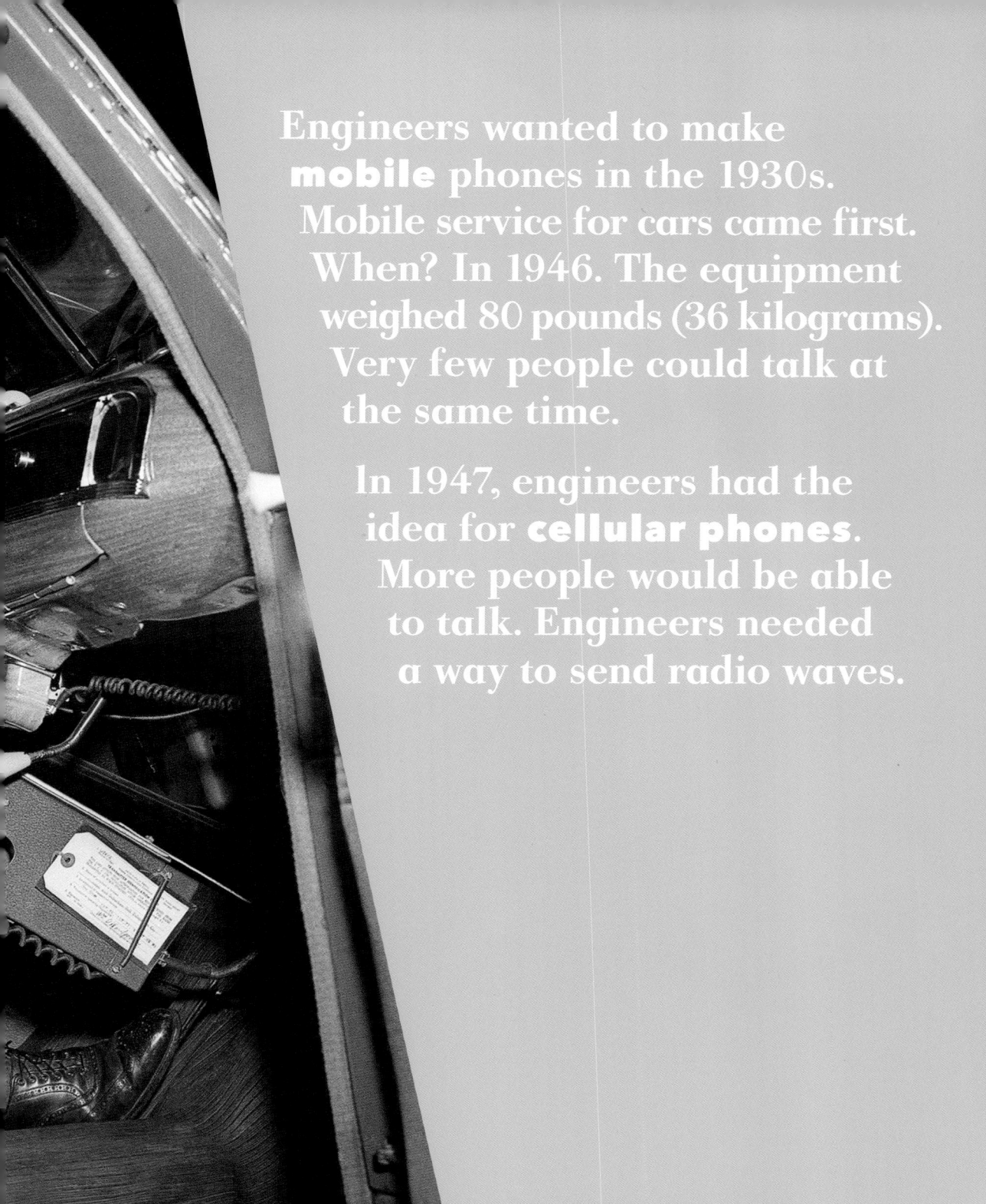

Engineers wanted to make **mobile** phones in the 1930s. Mobile service for cars came first. When? In 1946. The equipment weighed 80 pounds (36 kilograms). Very few people could talk at the same time.

In 1947, engineers had the idea for **cellular phones**. More people would be able to talk. Engineers needed a way to send radio waves.

Martin Cooper

Martin Cooper is an engineer. He worked for Motorola. It is a communications company. His team placed radio **transmitters** in New York. In 1973, he made the first cell phone call. To who? Someone at a **rival** company.

DID YOU KNOW?

About 7.5 billion people live on Earth. About 6 billion of us have access to cell phones. Only 4.5 billion have access to toilets. More people have access to cell phones than toilets!

CHAPTER 1

Parts to make the first phones were big. So the phones were big, too. Later, the parts got smaller. Cell phones got smaller, too. Now we do more on our phones. And we like big screens. Phones are big again.

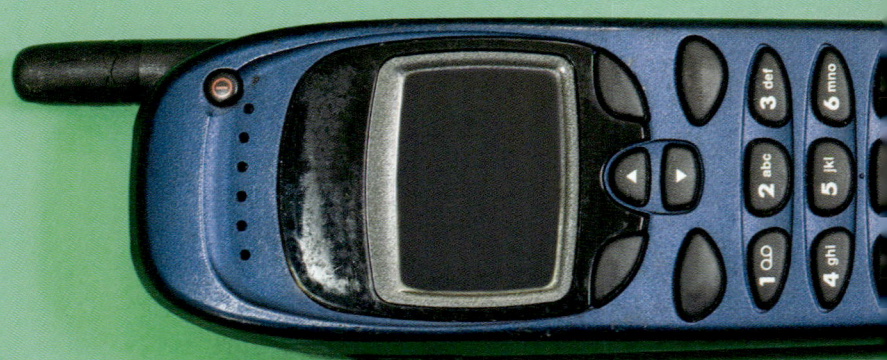

TAKE A LOOK!

The first phone was longer than a ruler. The battery took a long time to charge. Ten hours! See how the size of cell phones has changed over time.

1973 — TODAY

CHAPTER 1 — 11

CHAPTER 2
HOW THEY WORK

A cell phone is complex. Inside is a **circuit board**. It works as the brain. A battery provides power.

We tap a keyboard. It enters information. The liquid crystal display (LCD) is the screen.

CHAPTER 2

Cell phones work like radios. You speak into a microphone. The sound is changed into electrical signals. Transmitters send the signals as radio waves.

Phones have **receivers**. They get radio waves from other phones. These are changed back into sound. You hear the sound through a speaker.

> **DID YOU KNOW?**
>
> We can connect wirelessly with Wi-Fi. How? Wi-Fi also uses radio waves. They are transmitted through **routers**.

CHAPTER 3
A WORLD OF NETWORKS

How do we stay connected? Towers divide the world into cells. A cell is an area shaped like a **hexagon**. **Antennas** are on top of towers. Electronic equipment is at the base.

antenna

satellite phone

Some areas have no cell **network**. People use **satellite phones**. These send signals through satellites that orbit Earth.

CHAPTER 3 — 17

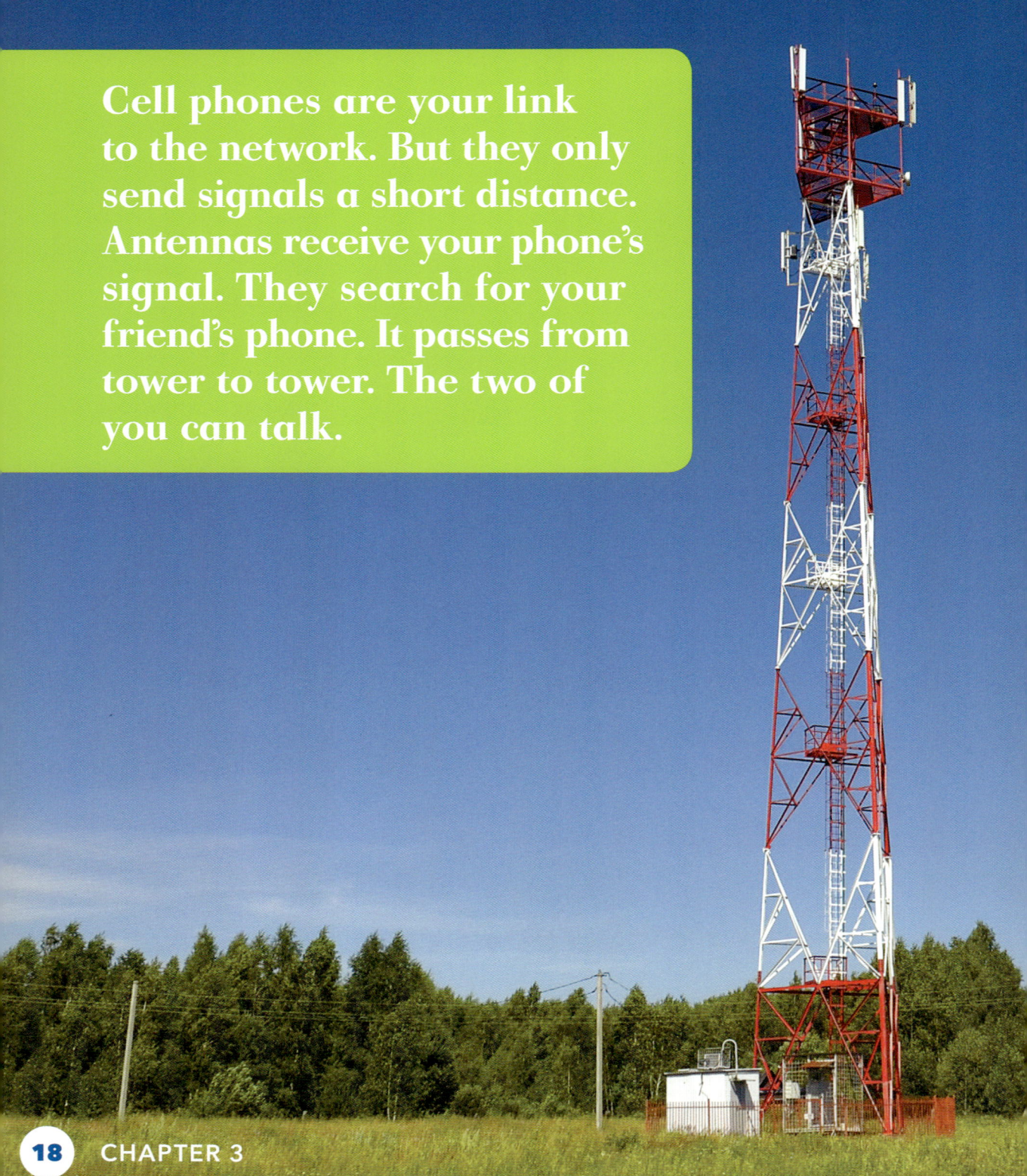

Cell phones are your link to the network. But they only send signals a short distance. Antennas receive your phone's signal. They search for your friend's phone. It passes from tower to tower. The two of you can talk.

TAKE A LOOK!

What happens if you are in a moving car? Calls are transmitted to different cells.

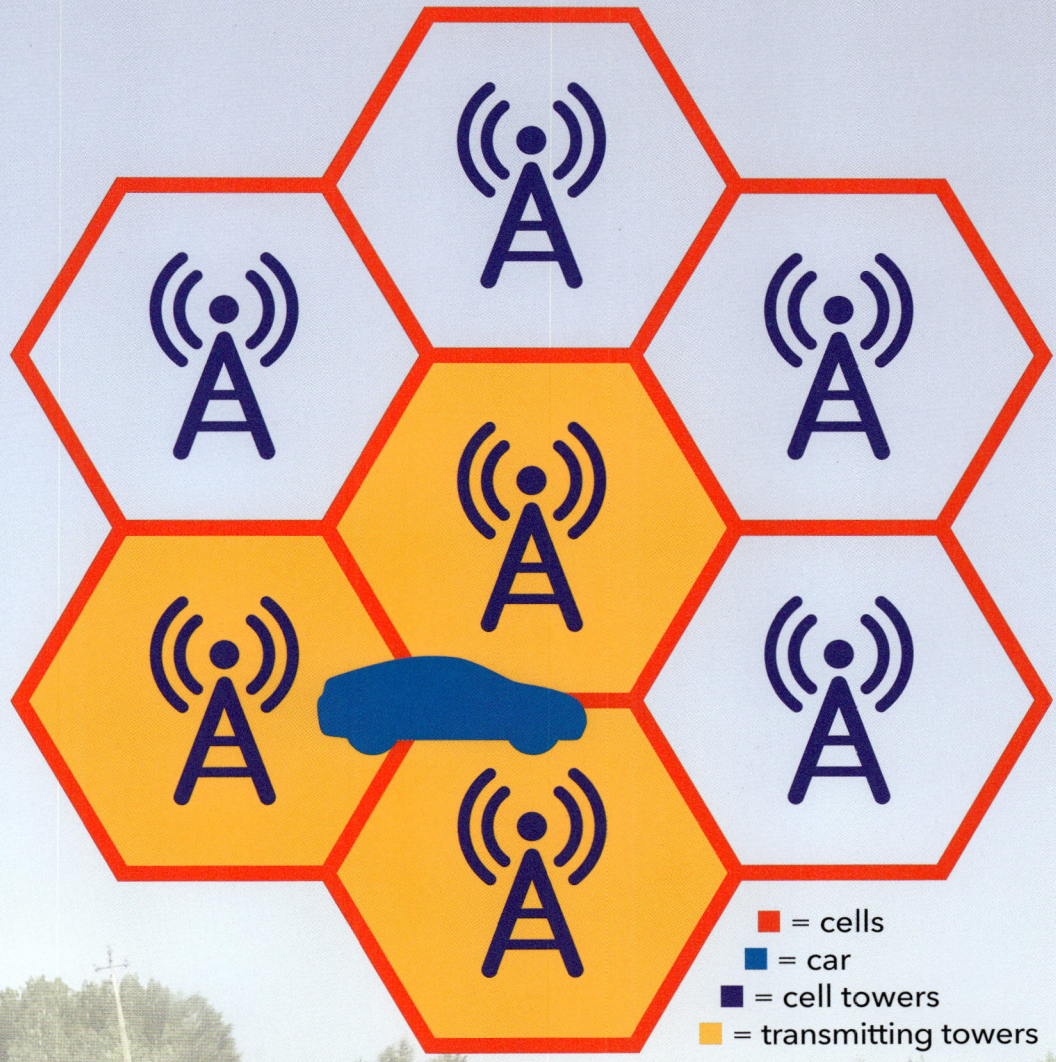

■ = cells
■ = car
■ = cell towers
■ = transmitting towers

CHAPTER 3 19

Cell towers are often hidden. They may be shaped like trees. Water tanks may have them. Can you spot a hidden tower?

Engineers had no idea how popular cell phones would become. We are connected in ways they never dreamed possible. How do cell phones affect you?

CHAPTER 3

ACTIVITIES & TOOLS

TRY THIS!

MAKE A CUP PHONE

Lines help carry sound, which makes phones without lines even more amazing. Try this activity to see how the vibrations of your voice travel through string.

What You Need:
- two paper or plastic cups
- pen
- string, up to 10 feet (3 meters) long

❶ Turn both cups upside down, with the opening facing down. Poke the pen through the center of the bottom of each cup.

❷ Poke one end of the string through the hole in the bottom of one cup. Tie a knot on the inside of the cup. Repeat with the second cup and other end of the string.

❸ Two people should each hold one cup and walk away from one another until the string is pulled tight.

❹ Keeping the string tight, one person should speak into the cup while the other person holds the cup to his or her ear to listen. What do you hear? Try it again keeping the string loose. What changes?

GLOSSARY

antennas: Metal devices, such as rods or wires, used to transmit and receive radio signals.

cellular phones: Wireless telephones that use radio waves over a networked area, or cells, and are served by towers at fixed points.

circuit board: A piece of plastic that has electrical circuits printed onto it in the form of small metal strips.

hexagon: A shape with six straight sides.

mobile: Able to move or be moved easily.

network: A communications system that transmits and receives within a geographic area.

receivers: Devices that pick up electrical signals and turn them into sound.

rival: One of two or more people or organizations who compete against one another.

routers: Devices that handle signals between networks.

satellite phones: Mobile phones that connect to orbiting satellites instead of land-based cell towers.

social media: Websites and apps that help people connect with one another.

transmitters: Electronic devices that send signals from phones.

INDEX

access 9
antennas 16, 18
battery 11, 12
cars 7
cells 16, 19
circuit board 12
Cooper, Martin 9
engineers 7, 9, 20
keyboard 13
liquid crystal display 13
microphone 14
Motorola 9
network 17, 18
New York 9
radio waves 7, 14
receivers 14
routers 14
satellite phones 17
size 10, 11
social media 5
speaker 14
towers 16, 18, 19, 20
transmitters 9, 14
Wi-Fi 14

TO LEARN MORE

Learning more is as easy as 1, 2, 3.
1) Go to www.factsurfer.com
2) Enter "cellphones" into the search box.
3) Click the "Surf" button to see a list of websites.

With factsurfer, finding more information is just a click away.